Strange Dances and Long Flights

A Book About Animal Behaviors

by Patricia M. Stockland
illustrated by Todd Ouren

Special thanks to our advisers for their expertise:

Zoological Society of San Diego
San Diego Zoo
San Diego, California

Susan Kesselring, M.A., Literacy Educator
Rosemount-Apple Valley-Eagan (Minnesota) School District

PICTURE WINDOW BOOKS
Minneapolis, Minnesota

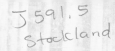

Managing Editor: Catherine Neitge
Creative Director: Terri Foley
Art Director: Keith Griffin
Editor: Christianne Jones
Designer: Todd Ouren
Page production: Picture Window Books
The illustrations in this book were prepared digitally.

Picture Window Books
5115 Excelsior Boulevard
Suite 232
Minneapolis, MN 55416
877-845-8392
www.picturewindowbooks.com

Printed in the United States of America.

Library of Congress Cataloging-in-Publication Data
Stockland, Patricia M.
Strange dances and long flights : a book about animal behaviors/
by Patricia M. Stockland ; illustrated by Todd Ouren.
p. cm. — (Animal wise)
Includes bibliographical references and index.
ISBN 1-4048-0936-8 (hardcover)
1. Animal behavior—Juvenile literature. I. Ouren, Todd, ill.
II. Title.

QL751.5.S758 2005
591.5—dc22   2004023308

Behavior Adaptations

Why do some animals act the way they do? Adaptation is the answer.

An animal can adapt by changing its behavior. By changing its behavior, the animal might be safer. It might even get a better meal.

Find out why some animals act so strangely and how different behaviors help animals survive.

Monarch Butterflies

The fall weather becomes cooler. Monarch butterflies begin their long flight.

Where are the monarchs going? They are starting their migration to Mexico. Winter in Canada is too hard on these butterflies. To cope with the cold, they fly south.

A single monarch butterfly doesn't live long enough to make the entire trip to Mexico and back. It takes five generations to make the full trip.

Cape Ground Squirrel

The hot sun bakes the African desert. The Cape ground squirrel burrows for seeds, leaves, and roots.

The Cape ground squirrel is able to stay in the heat with the help of its tail. The squirrel keeps its fluffy tail over its back. The tail serves as a sunshade, and the squirrel stays cool while it eats.

The Cape ground squirrel also uses its tail as a warning flag. When danger is near, the squirrel moves its tail up and down to tell others, "Watch out!"

Honeybee

The beehive is alive with action. A honeybee dances on the honeycomb.

This insect isn't dancing for fun. The dance shows other bees it is time to get to work. The dancing honeybee has found food. Its dance shows fellow workers where the food is located.

If the dance goes in a circle, food is close by. But if the honeybee makes a figure eight, the bees have farther to fly.

Baboon

The male baboon sits in the tall African grass. He lets out a big yawn.

A baboon's yawn doesn't mean the big animal is tired. By showing its terrifying teeth, the baboon is threatening another animal. This facial expression means, "I'm tough!" Predators and rivals know to back off.

Monkeys and apes use many facial expressions. These looks help the animals communicate and understand each other.

Leaf Insect

Warm breezes blow the leaves of a tree. The leaf insect sways on a branch.

This bug is an expert at camouflage. Not only does it look like a leaf, but it acts like one, too! When the leaves move, the leaf insect moves along with them. Birds and other predators don't notice it. If the bug is attacked, it drops to the ground like a falling leaf.

Some types of leaf insects are wrinkled so they look like dead leaves.

13

Great Horned Owl

Nighttime covers the forest in darkness. The great horned owl sits alert on its perch.

This large bird loves the dark. While other hunters sleep, this animal is getting ready to eat. Its sharp eyesight and hearing help the owl see small prey scurrying on the ground. Its soft feathers let the owl attack silently.

The owl's speckled brown feathers help it blend safely into the wooded surroundings while it sleeps during the day.

Sockeye Salmon

Red and green fish fill the river. The sockeye salmon swim upstream.

These fish make a long, hard journey to spawn. Salmon swim from the salty sea to freshwater lakes. They splash against strong river currents. The fish jump up rapids and over rocks to reach the final place to have their babies.

While they live in the sea, sockeye salmon are silver and steel-blue. But when they return to freshwater rivers to spawn, the fish turn bright red.

Western Fence Lizard

The sun warms a rough rock. The Western fence lizard basks in the heat.

This lizard isn't being lazy. It is lying on the rock to gather energy from the sun's rays. The little lizard can also see predators and prey better from the rock.

If a female comes near its rock, the male Western fence lizard will show off its bright blue, sometimes greenish, belly by doing push-ups.

Brown Bear

Cold air ruffles the brown bear's fur. It is time for a long winter nap.

Sometimes, the best behavior is none at all. During the summer, the brown bear ate a lot. That extra weight will help the bear survive the cold winter months. A long nap uses less energy than hunting for food in deep snow. The bear stays dormant in its cozy den.

During the winter, female bears give birth to their cubs.

Do You Remember?

Point to the picture of the animal described in each question.

1. My giant yawn doesn't mean I'm tired. I use it to tell others I'm tough. Who am I?

   (baboon)

2. I leave the salty sea and swim upstream to have my babies. Who am I?

   (sockeye salmon)

3. When I find a food source, I return to my hive. My special dance tells other workers which direction to fly. Who am I?

   (honeybee)

Fun Facts

Cape ground squirrels use their tails for shade only during the midday heat.

Male baboons often avoid fighting each other because their expressions are so clear. If a bigger, stronger male yawns at a rival, the rival knows to leave.

Leaf insects disguise their eggs as well as themselves. The bugs drop their eggs on the ground. There, the eggs look like seeds.

Animals that sleep during the day and hunt at night, such as the great horned owl, are called nocturnal.

Some sockeye salmon swim as far as 930 miles (1,488 kilometers) to reach their spawning grounds.

Glossary

adaptation—any change an animal makes to live or survive better in its environment

behavior—how an animal usually acts

burrows—digs

dormant—not active

generation—a line of offspring from a common family

migration—to move to a different area, usually for part of the year

predator—an animal that hunts and eats other animals

prey—an animal that is hunted by another animal for food

spawn—to mate and lay eggs

23

TO LEARN MORE

At the Library

Ganeri, Anita. *Animal Behavior.* Hauppauge, N.Y.: Barron's, 1992.

Gardner, Robert. *Science Project Ideas About Animal Behavior.* Springfield, N.J.: Enslow Publishers, 1997.

O'Hare, Jeffrey A. *Beastly Behaviors: Find the Baffling Bonds Between Amazing Animals.* Honesdale, Pa.: Boyds Mill Press, 2002.

On the Web

FactHound offers a safe, fun way to find Web sites related to this book. All of the sites on FactHound have been researched by our staff. www.facthound.com

1. Visit the FactHound home page.
2. Enter a search word related to this book, or type in this special code: 1404809368
3. Click the FETCH IT button.

Your trusty FactHound will fetch the best Web sites for you!

INDEX

Look for all of the books in the Animal Wise series:

Pointy, Long, or Round
A Book About Animal Shapes

Sand, Leaf, or Coral Reef
A Book About Animal Habitats

Stripes, Spots, or Diamonds
A Book About Animal Patterns

Red Eyes or Blue Feathers
A Book About Animal Colors

Strange Dances and Long Flights
A Book About Animal Behavior

Swing, Slither, or Swim
A Book About Animal Movements